THE COOLEST GOLF
ENCYCLOPEDIA
FOR KIDS...
AND EVEN ADULT GOLF BEGINNERS

The Coolest Golf Encyclopedia for Kids... and Even Adult Golf Beginners.
Cooolz Ltd., 2019. 40 p., illustrated.

ISBN 978-9934-19-139-8

Dear readers,

In this great book you will get to know golf, a magnificent game played by millions of people around the world.

You will learn the history of golf, along with its rules and terms.

And it is very likely that golf will become your favorite game for a lifetime!

Golf originated in the beautiful country of Scotland.

Scottish shepherds invented this wonderful game a long, long time ago. According to legend, they played a game very similar to modern golf, using their crooks to hit stones into rabbit burrows.

In 1457, King James II of Scotland banned his citizens from playing golf as he felt it was distracting them from their preparations for war.

Over time, golf earned royal favor because Mary, Queen of Scots became the first known female golfer.

The world-famous St. Andrews golf course, now known as the Old Course, opened in 1552 in St. Andrews, Scotland.

And now golf has conquered the world.

Golf has even been played in space! United States astronaut Alan Shepard used a golf club to hit the ball twice on the moon's surface on February 6, 1971.

People set up golf courses in the desert, in the mountains, in the middle of seas and oceans, and even in life-threatening places. Because nothing can beat their desire to play golf!

Although grass is present on most golf courses, it is not always necessary. For example, the staff and guests at Antarctic stations play golf on the snow.

Let's go on a tour of the golf course.

Are you ready? Our journey is a long one, stretching over many miles.

We can walk, or we can take a special golf car called a cart.

Either way, you'll enjoy being surrounded by nature.

This is a golf course. Beautiful, isn't it?

Take a look at the lovely scenery and the most important thing—the grass, which is a special type of grass you will not see anywhere else other than on a golf course, says the **greenkeeper** or course supervisor.

Yet a golf course is not just grass.

Look. What else can you see? Some weird stripes, ponds, sandpits, and nicely mown grass areas marked with flagsticks. So, let's see how it all works.

A golf course has holes. The **hole** itself is just an opening in the ground. However, for a golfer the hole is a target. The ball must be hit exactly into it.

Also, it is a long way to the hole from where you first hit the ball. Sometimes it is so far away that you can't even see the hole from the starting position.

Even if the golfers can't see the hole, they are able to aim at it because the hole is marked by a **flagstick**.

A golf course can have a total of nine or eighteen holes. Golf courses are like people: some are big and others are small.

Those enthusiastic people moving from one hole to another with bags full of clubs are **golfers**, the golf players. The golfers' way to the hole starts from a **tee**.

Tees vary in distance to the hole for women, men, seniors, professionals, and amateurs. In competitions for kids, tees are set closer to the hole.

A well-mown grass area with a hole and a flagstick in it is called a **green**.

The way from the tee to the hole is called a **fairway**.

This is also mown grass, but it is not as neat as the grass on the green. Hitting the golf ball along the fairway is the easiest way to reach the hole. Each hole on the course has a different distance from the tee to the hole, measured in yards.

The golfer faces many hazards on the golf course such as ponds, streams, tall grass, trees, and sand traps called **bunkers**.

The hazards are there to test the skill of the golfer.

The tall grass is called **rough**. The taller the grass is, the harder it is to hit the ball from it.

Usually golfers carry their clubs in large, heavy bags.

They can carry the bag over their shoulder, or put it on a special wheeled trolley, or they can take an assistant called a **caddie** to carry the bag.

The caddie's job is not just to carry the golfer's bag.

The caddie also helps make decisions and supports the player in difficult situations.

After all, anything can happen while you are playing through all eighteen holes.

So, friendly support and professional advice are necessary.

Every golf course has a cozy house called the **clubhouse**.

This is a place where golfers get together to meet with colleagues, chat about holes and strokes, share the latest news, discuss business, or just take a rest between holes or after a game.

Golfers practice their long strokes on a special area called a **driving range**.

The driving range is usually built on one level, but you can also come across driving ranges that have two or even three levels.

Short strokes are usually practiced on grass areas called **chipping greens** and **putting greens**.

There are an almost unimaginable number of golfers in the world, maybe even as many as one hundred million.

Originally, golf was a game played only by men, but women also learned to play and enjoy golf.

They can do it really well, as well as men.

It seems like everyone plays golf now: kings, businessmen and women, housewives, regular workers, writers, children, and the elderly.

And anyone can play it regardless of age, nationality, or language. It truly is a game for all that can be played for a lifetime.

Golfers hit the ball with **clubs**.

There are different types of club, and each club is meant to be used for a certain type of stroke.

The golfer chooses which club to use depending on the distance the ball needs to fly.

Let's meet the clubs:
Wood—club with a massive head for long strokes. Woods include the thick driver, which hits the ball much further than other clubs.
Iron—light club for strokes over a shorter distance than wood.
Wedge—club similar to the iron, but for short strokes from sand or grass.
Putter—club for rolling strokes (putt) on the green.

According to the rules, there must be no more than fourteen clubs in the golfer's bag.

A golfer must hit the ball from the tee into the hole with as few strokes as possible.

The player with the total lowest number of strokes after all holes have been played is the winner.

Now let's look at how scores are counted and what they are called.

The number of strokes a golfer usually needs to get from the tee to the hole is set for each hole. This standard is called **par**.

Depending on the distance from the tee to the hole, the par can be 3, 4, 5, or even 6 strokes on the very long golf holes.

Hole-in-One—the act of hitting the ball into the hole from the tee in one amazing stroke. This is the best possible score.
Birdie—counts as one stroke under (fewer than) par.
Eagle—counts as two strokes under par.
On long par 5 and par 6 holes, a golfer can make an **Albatross**—this counts as three strokes under par.

These are the scores of a very good game.

However, some scores may be worse.

Bogey—counts as one stroke over (more than) par.
Double Bogey—counts as two strokes over par.
Triple Bogey—counts as three strokes over par.

And so on.

Golfers write down their scores on specially designed cards called **scorecards**.

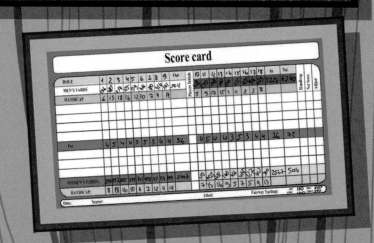

Let's get better acquainted with these scores. We can't see them, of course, but let's try to imagine what they might look like.

Par—the "gold standard." And he has an appropriately solid look: round like a ball, a black mustache, a bowtie, and a golden crown on his head.

Hole-in-One—King of luck and skill, he looks like a real pop star: a snow-white smile, a fur coat on his shoulders, a thick chain around his neck, and a crown of gold.

Birdie—she's a cool, brightly dressed, happy girl. Small birds of paradise begin to flutter around her and in her eyes when a player gets the ball into the hole with one stroke under par.

Eagle—his black hair and proud expression make him look like an eagle.

Albatross—he is dressed in an English suit and wears a bowler hat. He looks haughtily on everything that happens, like the big sea bird whose name he bears.

Hole-in-One, Birdie, Eagle, and Albatross are the **Great Golf Four**.

Bogey, **Double Bogey**, and **Triple Bogey** are worse scores, and they look appropriately bad. Like scarecrows.

According to the rules, every stroke is counted in golf, even if the player misses the ball completely or doesn't hit the ball properly.

Other strokes may also cause a variety of rule infringements and drops.

A drop is counted as an extra stroke, and takes place if the ball can't be hit from the place it falls, for example, if the ball lands in water or outside the golf course.

The ball is picked up (or a new one used if it's lost) and dropped in a place from where the game can continue.

An additional stroke is not counted if the ball hits an unnatural or temporary obstacle not installed by the course designer, for example, a road, an animal, or an area under repair.

If a player hits someone else's ball instead of his own, he will receive a two-stroke penalty.

The most severe penalty is for fraud or deliberate breaking of the rules—the player is banned from taking part in the competition.

There are a lot more rules in golf, of course. Here, we have just considered the ones that are needed to start playing.

It is not easy to remember all the rules, so you can ask for the official **rulebook** at the golf club.

Take the rulebook with you on the course and read it if there is any question about what to do in certain situations.

In a difficult situation during a competition, it is necessary to call the main **competition judge** or the **course marshal**. This professional knows the rules of golf better than anyone and always honestly resolves any dispute.

The oldest set of rules of golf was drawn up in 1744 by Edinburgh Golf Club.

As well as the official rules, there are rules about how to behave on the course. These rules are known as **golf etiquette**.

These rules are not at all complicated and they are based on the following principles: honesty, safety, respect for other players, attention to the speed of the game, care for the course, and respect for the employees.

These are the basic rules of golf etiquette:
• Always play and record your scores honestly.
• Do not change the position of the ball during the game.
• Play from the point where the ball fell.
• Shout "FORE!" if your ball might hit other people on the course.

- Do not hit the ball if other players are ahead of you.
- Do not talk while someone gets ready to hit the ball.
- Do not take too much time before hitting your ball.
- Do not stand on another player's stroke line on the green.
- Do not show negative emotions during the game. In other words, do not go crazy, do not break the stick, do not cry.
- Repair divots (lumps of torn-up grass and earth) on the course.
- Do not hit the grass unnecessarily.
- Be patient while a course attendant finishes a job.
- Wear appropriate golf clothing. 😊

But what is the main rule in golf?

Enjoy the golf course, companionship, and the game itself!

Play and win!

Not for the sake of winning, but for the love of golf!

Read about the exciting adventures of Hole-in-One, Albatross, Eagle, and Birdie in the real golf fairy tale PAR vs. Hole-in-One: The rescue of the Great Golf Four.

For more information follow www.cooolgolf.com.

CONTENTS

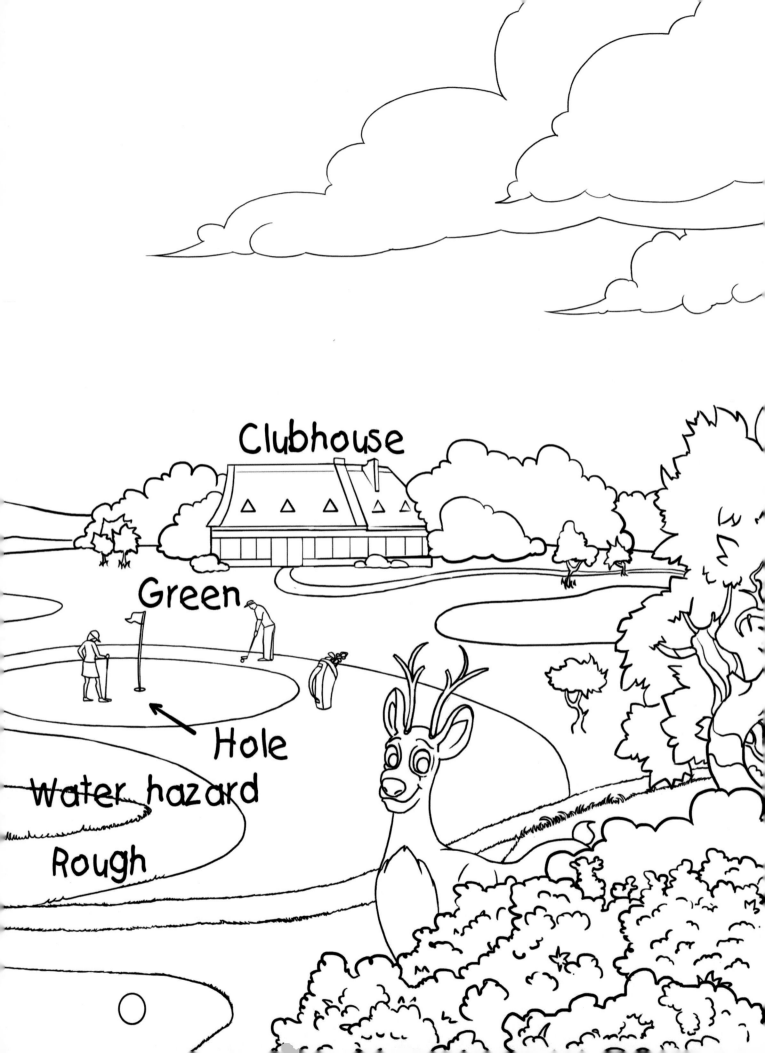

The Coolest Golf Encyclopedia for Kids...
and Even Adult Golf Beginners.

Cooolz Ltd., 2019. 40 p., illustrated.

ISBN 978-9934-19-139-8

Made in the USA
Middletown, DE
03 July 2023

34545779R00024